COME PLAY WITH ME

A Follett JUST Beginning-To-Read Book of Verse

COME PLAY WITH ME

Margaret Hillert

Illustrated by Kinuko Craft

FOLLETT PUBLISHING COMPANY
CHICAGO

ISBN 0-695-30587-5 Paper Binding
ISBN 0-695-40587-X Titan Binding

Library of Congress Catalog Card Number: 75-884

First Printing

COME PLAY WITH ME

My Dog and I

My dog can jump.

My dog can jump.

My dog can play and run.

And I can jump.

I like to jump.

My dog and I have fun.

7

My Playhouse

I have a little playhouse—
Yellow, red, and blue.
I like it in my playhouse,
And you will like it, too.

8

Not That

Mother said, "Oh no, oh no!

Up and up and up you go

To look at something little and brown.

I want you to get down, get down."

9

The Red Car

A little red car
Is fun for play.
Get in. Get in
And ride away.

10

Guess

Guess who it is.

Guess who. Guess who.

One looks like me.

One looks like you.

But you look funny.

I do, too.

Up

Up I go.

Look and see.

Up, up, up.

What fun for me.

My Baby

I play with my baby,
And you can play, too.
I look like a mother.
Now what can we do?

13

A Ball

Up and down.

Up and down.

A ball can go up.

A ball can come down.

Fun with Father

Father, Father,

Run, run, run.

I like to play with you.

What fun.

My Book

I like to look

In a book, book, book

To see what I can see.

A book is fun.

Now you get one

And see what you can see.

16

The Boat

Oh, oh, oh.

The boat can go.

Go, go, go.

Little boat, go.

Play

"Here is something blue.

Here is something red.

You can have fun with two.

Go play," my mother said.

18

Little Ones

Come look at this.

Come look and see.

Something little—

One, two, three.

Work

I like to help my mother work.

My mother likes it, too.

I like to help my father work.

Here's something I can do.

Jump

Jump a little.

Jump a little.

One, two, three.

Jump a little.

Jump a little.

Play with me.

Ride

I like to ride. Do you?

I like to ride with you,

With you and my dog, Mike.

That is what I like.

A Penny

What will you do

With a penny for you?

With one little penny,

What will you do?

Jump In

Oh, my. Oh, my.

I guess that I

Will jump in here

And play. Oh, my.

24

Look for Me

One, two, three.

Come look for me.

Did you find my spot?

No, you did not.

Cookies

My mother said to help.

Now see what we can do

With cookies, cookies, cookies

For me and you and you.

Big Me

Come here. Come here.

Come here and see.

What fun. What fun.

A big, big me.

Come Play with Me

Twenty-one rhymes with charming illustrations provide an introduction to verse for the youngest readers. The verses employ a vocabulary of 75 preprimer words.

Word List

7	my		mother		do
	dog		said	**12**	see
	and		oh		what
	I		no	**13**	baby
	can		up		with
	jump		go		now
	play		look(s)		we
	run		at	**14**	ball
	like(s)		something		come
	to		brown	**15**	father
	have		want	**16**	book
	fun		get	**17**	boat
8	playhouse		down	**18**	here
	a	**10**	the		two
	little		car	**19**	this
	yellow		is		three
	red		for	**20**	work
	blue		ride		help
	it		away	**22**	Mike
	in	**11**	guess	**23**	penny
	you		who	**25**	did
	will		one(s)		find
	too		me		spot
9	not		but	**26**	cookies
	that		funny	**27**	big

Uses of These Books. These books are planned for the very youngest readers, those who have been learning to read for about six to eight weeks and who have a small preprimer reading vocabulary. The books are written by Margaret Hillert, a first-grade teacher in the Royal Oak, Michigan, schools. Each book is illustrated in full color.

Because of their high interest and readability, these books are ideal for independent reading by primary and pre-primary children—at school, in the library, and at home. The books may also be incorporated into the basic reading program to develop children's interests, expand their vocabularies, and improve word-attack skills. It has been suggested that they might serve as the foundation for a skillfully directed reading program.

Careful attention is given to vocabulary load and sentence length, but the first criterion is interest to children. They will read *JUST Beginning-To-Read* books with confidence, with success, and with real enjoyment.